A Ligature for Black ~~Bodies~~

I was totally won over when
I read the manuscript for
Denise Miller's *A Ligature for
Black Bodies*, which I think can't
arrive a moment too soon. So
many of these poems reminded
me of the lynch poems of
Sterling A. Brown – Miller's
writing's their own, but it taps
into the craziness, the wild
destruction of the Black body
for any reason, and the many
ways the explanations of these
murders try to be rational, and
justified. In these powerful and
necessary poems, Denise Miller
has lyrically sketched out the
madness.

— CORNELIUS EADY
John C, Hodges Chair of Excellence
The University of Tennessee/Knoxville

A
Ligature
For
Black
~~Bodies~~

Denise Miller

First published in 2021
by Black Spring Press Group
Suite 333, 19-21 Crawford Street
Marylebone, London W1H 1PJ
United Kingdom

Edited by Cornelius Eady
Cover design and typeset by Edwin Smet

The right of Denise Miller to be identified as author of
this work has been asserted in accordance with section 77
of the Copyright, Designs and Patents Act 1988

ISBN 978-1-913606-18-3

*The editor has generally followed American spelling and punctuation
at the author's request.*

BLACKSPRINGPRESSGROUP.COM

Denise Miller is a professor, poet and mixed media artist whose poetry has been published in the *Offing*, *African American Review* and *Blackberry: A Magazine*. They were named the 2015 Willow Books Emerging Poet, an AROHO Waves Discussion Fellowship awardee, a finalist for the Barbara Deming Money for Women Fund, and a Hedgebrook Fellow. Their work titled *Core* was released by Willow Books in 2015 and has since been nominated for a 2016 American Book Award and a 2016 Pushcart Prize. Miller has been named a 2016 William Randolph Hearst Fellow at the American Antiquarian Society. Their chapbook *Ligatures* was published in 2016 by Rattle Press. Most recently, they have been awarded a 2020 Storyknife Residency and a 2020 Martha's Vineyard Institute of Creative Writing Fellowship. Their pronouns are they/them. More of their work can be found at www.denisemiller.studio

TABLE OF CONTENTS

Author's note:

When I originally wrote this manuscript, it was 2016 and the murders of too many Black people to mention even then left me with the image of Black bodies falling like trees being cut down in a forest. The image and the ensuing emotion fit for me then – so the title *A Ligature for Black Bodies* also fit. However, now with the current murders of Breonna Taylor and George Floyd among so many others, I realize the life-threatening danger in calling Black people bodies.

We are not bodies, only.
We are not bodies, only.
WE. ARE. NOT. BODIES. ONLY.

However, in the current discourse about Black people and police brutality, many of us use "Black bodies" to describe Black people. Although this language clearly reflects the physicality of the overwhelming numbers of us we see felled by police bullets and knees and arms yearly, monthly, weekly and even daily in this country, this seemingly benign act of separating body from breath or body from spirit is a revelatory reminder of the mind/body problem that Black people have been historically forced to reckon with since the first enslaved "negroes" were brought to Massachusetts in 1624. From these beginnings, a white power structure has always sought to make bodies out of Black people and, because of a racially rooted power structure set up to create and perpetuate racism, we Black people have much too often had to reclaim these bodies that have been systematically stripped of breath.

Our current striving in this country to convince that same power structure that Black Lives matter, will not keep Black bodies from falling until this same white power structure sees that we are Black people (whole, living, breathing) and that the same animating principles that make them human are the same animating principles that make us human. This is how they have and continue to make us bodies when they refuse to see us as human. So it is up to us, Black people, to name our humanness as part of a long line of ancestors beginning I know before Frederick Douglass and Sojourner Truth, through Maime Till Mobley and Sandra Bland, all the way to our Black and Trans brothers and sisters, and I hope to and through these poems in these pages. This book then, is *A Ligature for Black*, a song, a litany, and a reckoning for all that we were, are, and will become.

This was a horrible event.

It should not happen again, and there already have been lessons learned and that is the positive side of this tragedy.

Already, steps have been taken to assure that these events do not reoccur:
- The city has bought body cams for all its officers. That will help.
- Dash cams are on the way for CPD and suburban departments using $1 million that our office has seized from criminals.

— Excerpt from "The entire statement read by Prosecutor McGinty in the Tamir Rice Case as quoted in Officers Will Not Be Charged in Tamir Rice Shooting Death" POSTED 1:02 PM, DECEMBER 28, 2015, BY DARCIE LORENO, JEN STEER, PEGGY GALLEK AND ED GALLEK

Dear Spectators,

You will need a context for viewing – so first,
consider the noose, that birthmarked
ligature on brailled, brown bodies with retinas
fingerlike, trace postcarded necks of bodies

born brown then noosed, born brown then picnic
blackened, born brown & then trophied
into ear or penis or vagina or tongue –
born brown & biologied into body

cam-ed bodies born brown then bulleted, born brown
then broken, born brown then bent –
born brown then esophagus-threaded through handcuff
born brown then bracketed by [hashtag & period].

Then period turns to question marked silhouette – her
2015 body, hangs – her standing kneel, bracketed by bars
looks so much like pause between prayer & dancing –
looks so much like a 1913 3 & ¼ by 5 cardboarded brown

body with soul smoking skyward, looks so much like *alive, soaked in
coal oil before being set on fire* * – this reverse alchemy
a living brown body, all slick & shine then, dissolution – a not so
mysterious transmuting, bone to blood to ash – &

2015 and 16 look so much like 1910 –
See the silhouetted corpses of African Americans shot from
a 1920 Kodak, shot on a 1982 Sony, shot on a 2015 dash cam,
shot on a 2016 body cam.

– shot

or dragged
or tased
or cuffed
or pounded against pavement –

these bodies born brown then catapulted into lifeless silent
film stars – surrounded by spectators.

* Bennie Simmons, alive, soaked in coal oil before being set on fire. June 13,
1913. Anadarko, Oklahoma. Gelatin silver print. Real photo postcard. 31/4 x
5 in. Etched into negative, "Edies Photo Anadarko Oklo"
www.withoutsanctuary.org/main.html

Offense

The alleged offense of the African American killed is in parentheses at the
beginning of each poem in this section. These "confession" poems are meant
to be in the voices of the police officers and are taken from and inspired by
news articles and their police reports after the incidents. The found poems
are in the form of lune and are found poems from these primary sources and
are used to set the context before each police officer's confession.

And Everybody Thought I Was Racist –
a lune found poem

Slager / his lawyer — a defense:
"Didn't know Scott
was unarmed." Felt threatened quick

decision to shoot because he
believed Scott
might pull a gun and

shoot him first.

— found from "Michael Slager, Cop Who Killed Walter Scott,
Says He Felt Threatened" By Craig Melvin

Next to Scott's Body, An Officer's Confession

– for Walter Scott

(His brake light was out)

       Him. Hands cuffed.
Me, bent and bending. Dropping taser. I lie.

– he lies. Body down. Flesh pitted by five of my service
pistol's eight bullets.

           Difference is, I lie for a reason.

A white man, hand hugging gun hot as an open mouth, legs
running toward me is less-threatening than a black man
running away – his hands molded into batonless fists – torso
folded at waist, legs keeping pace like the last leg of a relay.

           C'mon. Say you wouldn't be scared
too.

dashcam video shows: – a lune/found poem kinda remix

McDonald walking down South
Pulaski a knife
in his hand, but strolling

away from officers when Van Dyke
jumps out of
his vehicle — pulls his gun.

Van Dyke began firing six seconds
after arriving took
15 seconds to fire 16

shots.

— found from "The killing of Laquan McDonald: The dashcam video vs.
police accounts" By Wayne Drash, CNN

13 Seconds on Pulaski, Another Officer's Confession

— for Laquan McDonald

(He punctured the tires of a car with his knife)

And shit yeah, I'm scared   of any black boy's moving —
his marking a deliberate line through my world.

so I set that body spinning   — a black top through
thinning air —

        13 seconds   from start to
    motionless. He's holed and I'm the empty chamber,
wholly intent on reloading.

He's Heard Saying – a lune/found poem kinda remix

"I can't breathe, I can't
breathe" as officer
Pantaleo places him in chokehold

Garner goes into cardiac arrest.
EMS workers arrive –
do not appear to administer

CPR. Garner is pronounced dead.

– found from "VIDEO: Man Dies During Arrest for Selling Illegal
Cigarettes, NYPD Says" By Nicholas Rizzi and Aidan Gardiner

What I Learned at the Academy, Another Officer's Confession

– for Eric Garner

(He was illegally selling cigarettes.)

It was never supposed to be a chokehold.
Just a wrestling move I learned at the
Academy. So, I locked one arm under
his, slipped the other around his torso –

how else to let him know there is no sense in resisting?
– just let me tip the perp, make him lose his balance.

            Just let me ground him.

More choke than hold, my arm – the sound of begging,
            his breath – his head to concrete, my right arm

around his thick of neck.

Breaking – a found poem

1.

Ard's cruiser dragged Victor, nearly
breaking him in
half. When the car stopped –

in parking lot, Ard called
for an ambulance
jumped out of the car,

yelling, "Dude, you all right?
Are you alive?
You hear me?"

2.

Victor's mother – so grief-stricken her knees kept
buckling, she had to be

held up by two friends.
One told her:
"Look at all these different

people coming together for Victor."
"Yes, yes, I
know," she sobbed, "but it

hurts too much."

3.

The day after the funeral, TV news was
about to report that a

paramedic had found a gun in Victor's pocket.
A video, taken from the

dashboard of another officer's car, recorded what happened
in the minutes before discovery:

Three officers squatted next to
Ard's car, looking
under it at Victor. Ard

unlocked the passenger side of
his car — got
something out. The object is

light-colored and floppy, but isn't
clearly visible. Ard,
holding the object, crawled under

the car next to Victor's
body — stayed there
for 40 seconds. Two minutes

later, paramedics found a 9mm
silver and black
semi-automatic in Victor's pocket.

Lab tests showed the gun
had been wiped
clean. No fingerprints on it —

not Victor's, not anyone's.

— found from "Death of teen on bike shows risks of expanded use of Tasers"
By Meg Laughlin

Click-Click, Another Officer's Confession

– for Victor Steen

(... had seen him at a construction site and thought he may have
stolen something. Or he didn't have a light on his bike – only two
reflectors.)

       Something shapes him into that
       smoke-slippery shadow I just
       saw shift from construction site
       to concrete. Not my fault he
       won't stop, I try to bull-horn
him to his feet.

Not sure if it is all my steel
and four wheels barreling after his two that make
his black body all limbed motion – but I know it's
the *click-click* split from taser to his skin through
that Florida night –

sound all snake's rattle – shock that follows bite –
that'll hurtle him from spin to flight to motionless

– A chassied tree branch.
            A tangle of dogwood or willow –

He lies. I slide under, lie –
next to him. Look the length of
axle to oil pan, then glide my
hand into his pocket – gift him
steel and lead.

                    Difference is –

I lie for a reason.

I Was Trained – a lune found poem

I kept my eyes on
suspect the entire
time. I was fixed on

his waistband and hand area.
I was trained   keep my
eyes on his

hands because "hands may kill."   The
male appeared   over 18 years old,
about

185 pounds. Based on "tap-tap"   training,
I shot...

– found from "I, Timothy Loehmann, state the following"

We Are Taught, Another Officer's Confession

-- for Tamir Rice

(a Black Male, camouflage hat, grey jacket, and black
sleeves at or near the swing set waving a gun and pointing at
people)

See, we were trained to keep eyes on hands —
we were trained that hands may kill — we were
                    trained to tap-tap

a hole as round as an open mouth — trained
to watch as nickel-tipped teeth tear through
a torso of grown flesh to leave an openness all

clean-edged

                                        — and gaping

but we were not taught to decipher a black
boy's body from the bulk of a black man.
Were taught to fix on the hands without reading for

wrinkle or smooth. We were taught to look
at the elbow, wait for when it begins to pendulum
toward our ticking hearts. We were taught to

shoot and move. We were taught that the
car is a coffin. We put his sister there to wait.

The Child [in the back seat] Was Unharmed –
a lune found poem

The office of the District
of Columbia medical
examiner said one round struck

Carey in the left side
of the back
of her head, and she

was also hit three times
in the back –
once in her left arm.

– found from "Woman killed during D.C. chase was shot five times from
behind, autopsy shows" By Steve Almasy

Can I Tell You What I Thought? Another Officer's Confession

> – for Miriam Carey and her 1-year-old daughter who was
> in the backseat of the car

(She ran in to a White House barrier with her car.)

Let me tell ya, she started it. Shit, they
teach us we're never off duty. Dust
clears and I don't wanna be the one
who didn't flip fear into instinct. Look –

if you're smart, you'd think:
anything can be a weapon, steel
or skin – then you wouldn't
question my bike rack to her
car's body, once, then again –

                              you wouldn't
                    – question

how hotly we pursued her.

After They Fatally Shot Her – a lune found poem

Louisville police officers serving the
no-knock search warrant
at Breonna Taylor's apartment the

night she died were told
her home was
a "soft target" with minimal threats,

and that the 26-year-old emergency
room technician was
likely home alone. "They said

they did not believe she
had children or
animals, but they weren't sure,"

Sgt. Jonathan Mattingly told investigators
in a recorded
interview almost two weeks after

police fatally shot Taylor in
her apartment. "Said
she should be there alone

because they knew where their target was."

– found from "Police interviews say Breonna Taylor's home was a 'soft
target,' suspect already located" by Tessa Duvall and Darcy Costello

They Knew – Another Officer's Confession

- For Breonna Taylor

(Authorities suggested that the actual subject of their
narcotics investigation was using her residence to get mail,
and store drugs and money)

They told us she was
                a target –
soft enough to warrant warning
before battering   ram, but hard
enough to tender   22 bullets   to
break   the black
of body and night.

Huh? – a found poem

Derek Chauvin:
Quit talking. Sit down. Is
he going to
jail? Get him down on

the ground. You got a
restraint? Hobble? Okay
you're under arrest guy. That's

why you're going to jail.
All right, you're
doing a lot of talking.

We'll hold him until EMS shows up.

George Floyd:
Please. Please let me stand.

Derek Chauvin:
No. Nope, just leave them.
Just leave them
Relax. Uh-huh. Uh-huh. You're a

lot of talking, a lot
of yelling. Takes
a heck of a lot

of oxygen to say that.
No, leave him.
Staying put where we got

him. That why we got the ambulance coming.

Male 3:
Check his pulse.
Check his.
Check his pulse.
Check his pulse.

Thomas Lane:
You got one?

J. Alexander Kueng:
I can't find one.
Derek Chauvin:
Huh?

– found from George Floyd Arrest Transcript Filed in District Court State
of Minnesota 7/7/2020 11:00 AM

Staying Put Where We Got Him –
Another Officer's Confession

– For George Floyd

(someone called 911 and reported that a man bought
merchandise... with a counterfeit $20 bill)

Takes a heck of a lot
of training to take the neck –
turn it – a heck of a lot
of self-restraining to not break
the neck – Can't you see, he earned it?

He's clogging the system with
his contraband and counterfeit.
So, I'm cleaning up the streets
with his body – bent and expending.
Why should I care he's trembling?

I hold even if he begs for breath
til his tongue touches pavement. Not
my fault this concrete is his death-bed.
His counterfeit $20 bought and paid for it.

He's criminal and my knee is his correction.

the 5 w's

That's Why – a mashup/lune/found poem kinda remix

A North Charleston police officer
felt threatened last
weekend when the driver he

stopped for a broken brake   light
tried to   overpower him, take his
Taser.

That's why Patrolman 1st Class
Michael Slager, former
Coast Guardsman, fatally shot 50-year-old

Walter Scott in the back.

– found from "Attorney: North Charleston police officer felt threatened
before fatal shooting" By Andrew Knapp and "Walter Scott Shooting:
What We Know About Officer Michael Slager" By Cassandra Vinograd

He, Quote "Felt Threatened" End Quote – a reporter's defense

– for Walter Scott

Who? –   a veteran of the police force, 1st
      class,
last person I'd expect to dishonorably
discharge his fear. See, here

I column them up. Blue slacks shadowing black, both margin
measured and integrity-stacked
      – just the facts.

      That background I dug under so
much life to find, that's – how I like to
write the truth.

If – a found poem

I.

If

they are found
to have lied
about the details

If

something comes back
that they lied purposely
misrepresented

the superintendent wants
to make clear he will seek
their termination

2.

The two cops, Detective
David Marsh and Officer
Joseph Walsh, were placed

40

on desk duty. Walsh was the
partner of Officer Jason Van
Dyke, who faces first-degree

murder charges for shooting
Laquan 16 times in 2014.
Walsh backed up Van Dyke's

version of events that don't jibe
with the shooting caught on the
now-viral dashcam video.

3.

Van Dyke said that Laquan, 17
had swung a knife at him, a
claim the video does not support.

Marsh, lead detective on the case,
signed off the reports – the dash
cam video "was viewed – found

to be consistent with accounts
of all witnesses," police reports.
The reports were also approved

by Lt. Anthony Wojcik, who
supervised the case. Marsh,
Walsh and Wojcik were all

called to testify before
a grand jury related to the
shooting of Laquan.

4.

At the time, the police spokesman
said it was "premature to speculate
on any action against the officers"

due to ongoing disciplinary
investigations which had been "held
pending the outcome" of the criminal

investigation that lead to murder
charges against Van Dyke. That
position changed shortly after

Escalante received and reviewed
the city inspector general's memo –
which was a preliminary suggestion

rather than a final ruling on whether
the accused officers violated Rule 14,
a provision in the police code related

to making false statements, written
or oral. Two other officers at the
scene who claimed to witness Van Dyke

shooting Laquan — Dora Fontaine
and Ricardo Viramontes — each
gave official statements of how events

transpired appeared to contradict
events caught on dashcam video.
Viramontes and Fontaine each said

Laquan ignored verbal direction
to drop the knife and instead raised
his right arm toward officer Van Dyke

"as if attacking Van Dyke." Fontaine
reported that Van Dyke fired in rapid
succession "without pause." Viramontes

added that Laquan "fell to the ground
but continued to move attempting to
get back up, with the knife still in his

hand... and Van Dyke fired his weapon
at [Laquan] McDonald continuously
until McDonald was no longer moving."

5.

The dashcam video showed
Laquan walking away from
Van Dyke when the shooting

43

started, and the injured teen
didn't appear to try to get back
up after he fell to the ground.

Both Viramontes and Fontaine
remain on unrestricted full duty.

– found from "Fire Officers If They Lied About Laquan Shooting,
Police Supt. Says" By Mark Konkol and Paul Biasco | January 22, 2016

I Believe Our Duty Is to Illuminate –
a lune found poem

Our reporters have been looking
into Tamir's background
see if he lived life

exposed to violence that could
explain why it
might be normal for him

to randomly aim what looks
like a real
gun in a public place.

– from "Our stories on Tamir Rice are the latest in the Northeast Ohio
Media Group's examination of how Cleveland police use force" By Chris
Quinn, Vice President of Content, Northeast Ohio Media Group

We've Kept the Focus On – another news media's defense

– for Tamir Rice

Where –   did you think he was
going to play? His momma and
daddy so twisted up in the system –
there is no way Tamir wasn't
destined to headline.

Don't whine – all that detail we detailed   after:
park bench,
        toy gun,   police
procedure,   a   dead
son –

        Look –

we were writing about
                        a 12-year-old

        black

                                        boy

.

A Gun and No Prints – a lune found poem

1. Planting

The object is light-colored, floppy
but isn't clearly
visible. Ard, holding the object,

crawled under the car next
to Victor's body
and stayed there for 40 seconds.

2. Burying

Victor's family, as well as
his pastors and
friends, were aghast. Victor was

scared of guns, they said.
He would not
have carried a gun around.

Lawson, FDLE investigator, was suspicious
enough of what
he had seen in video

to ask the four-year officer
about it. "Did
you put that gun on

Victor Steen?" Lawson asked in
a taped interview.
Ard answered no, the investigator

changed the subject.

– found poem from "Death of teen on bike shows risks of expanded use of
Tasers" By Meg Laughlin

Change the Subject – an investigator's confession

– for Victor Steen

When –

> he answers *no* –
> it's my signal to shift
>
> gaze at the dashcam   not
> like it's a spliced
> celluloid
>
> – birth-of-a-nation – remix
>   but to fix my eyes on
> the script.   Know what directing
> means?

40 seconds is plenty of time
to edit the bloopers.

What the Witnesses Say: a found poem

– for Miriam Carey

David, let's begin with you in Washington, D.C.
Describe that day, the day that, if we all sort of
remember back, we probably have heard about. It was
an amazing moment that ended with – what was it?
A standing ovation on the floor of the
House of Representatives for the Secret Service?

DAVID MONTGOMERY(DM):
That's exactly right. It was a fall day, October 3rd.
If you remember, the capital was already edgy,
because just a week or so before, there had been the
Navy yard shooting, so everyone was a little bit
jittery. At about – exactly 2:13 p.m., Miriam Carey
drives up to the – one of the White House security
checkpoints, with her 13-month-year-old
baby in back, and goes through that kiosk.

There's no gate there.

There's no barrier to ram.

She went past a kiosk, was ordered by the
Secret Service agents to stop, and she didn't.
She made a U-turn and tried to exit. And that's
when an off-duty Secret Service agent tried to

put up a sort of a bicycle rack-like fence to keep
her in. And she did not stop. She sort of
hit that, ran that gate, and continued —

AMY GOODMAN(AG):
Well, wait, wait. Just on that point, he put
up a fence after she drove there to keep
her in? Was he in uniform?

DM:
He was not in uniform. He was off-duty, and he
was carrying a cooler that you can — with we don't
know what was inside — that you can see in pictures.

AG:
You mean like a beer cooler?

DM:
Well, or a lunch cooler. We
don't know what it was.

AG:
So a man —

DM:
We don't know what was inside it.

AG:

So a man — all she saw, with her baby in
the back seat, is she has come into this
area, and a man has put up a fence against
her, and he's carrying a cooler.

DM:

Yes, yes.

AG:

So she pushes through that, and that's the first
ramming of a barrier that we heard about that day?

DM:

She actually, according to one witness, first tried to
steer around it. And then, apparently, the man, the
off-duty officer, repositioned it in front of her.

After Striking – an officer's declaration

– for Miriam Carey

Why? –

would she hit that barricade – why would
she make her car   stone
then sling it?

didn't she know that if some
kind of god
hadn't stopped him – goliath would
have taken david out?

Verdict

Charleston – a lune found poem

— for Walter Scott

A former South Carolina police
officer charged in
the videotaped killing of an

unarmed black motorist last April
is free on
bond after a judge ruled

that he shouldn't remain jailed
until his planned
October trial. Michael Slager is

charged with murder in the
shooting death of
Walter Scott. Slager is shown

on cellphone video firing eight
times as Scott
ran from a traffic stop

in North Charleston, S.C. The
case added fuel
to an already intense national

debate about how blacks are
treated by white
police officers. Slager, 34, had

been jailed in isolation for
more than eight
months since his arrest, *The Post*

and *Courier* reported last month.
His defense team
in December asked Circuit Judge

Clifton Newman to set his
trial for spring.
But prosecutor Scarlett Wilson is

also prosecuting the case of
Dylann Roof, the
white suspect in the killings

of nine black parishoners at
a Charleston church —
that trial is slated to

take place in July. Wilson
said a state
Supreme Court order prevents her

from trying other cases before
that one. His
attorneys asked the judge to

free him, saying he would
otherwise face 11
more months of incarceration.

– found from "Ex-cop in S.C. shooting of unarmed black motorist free on
bond" – by Greg Toppo

Over 400 Days – a found poem

– for Laquan McDonald

Petitioners For An Independent Prosecutor,
by their undersigned attorneys, respectfully
petition this Court for entry of an order finding
that Cook County State's Attorney Anita Alvarez
is disqualified from representing the People in connection

with the prosecution of Chicago Police Officer Jason Van Dyke
as any ongoing or future investigation and prosecution of the
Chicago Police officers who participated in the falsification
of reports, the destruction of evidence, the manipulation and
coercion of witnesses and other possible misconduct in the
aftermath of the fatal shooting of Laquan McDonald.

In support, Petitioners state:

A videotape of the fatal shooting of Laquan McDonald has gone
viral. The video unambiguously shows Mr. McDonald being
shot as he walks away from police officers and then shot again
and again as he lies motionless on the ground.

The video's anticipated release appears to have caused Cook
County State's Attorney Anita Alvarez to charge Chicago
Police Officer Jason Van Dyke with murder. Although the
State's Attorney had access to the video from day one of her
investigation, she allowed over 400 days to pass before

initiating the murder charges. Hours before the public release of the video (per the order of a Cook County judge), the State's Attorney finally charged Van Dyke.

This timing has produced an unprecedented crisis of confidence in the State's Attorney and her office. As this Petition explains, it appears that officers of the Chicago Police Department intimidated witnesses, manufactured witness statements, destroyed evidence, prepared false police reports, and may have provided false grand jury testimony as part of a concerted effort to portray Mr. McDonald's shooting not as it was, but as an act of heroic self-defense in response to Mr. McDonald's aggression toward Van Dyke and the other officers.

Many in the public believe that the State's Attorney was willing to adopt this false narrative; that she would have declined to file charges against Mr. Van Dyke if authorities had not been forced by court order to release the video; and that she only reversed course to avoid the certainty of public outrage after the video became available.

One thing is certain: but for the fortuity that Mr. McDonald's shooting was captured on videotape, there would be no charges against Officer Van Dyke. The false account of Mr. McDonald's death in the police records would be held up as "truth." Van Dyke would be portrayed as a hero. Mr. McDonald's shooting would be deemed a justified response to the fiction of his crazed attack on the officers. All of this – but for the video – would have been enabled by the lies in the police officers' official reports.

– found from Petition to Appoint Special Prosecutor Laquan McDonald

Unreasonable – a found poem mashup

— for Eric Garner

I. The Law

Was there probable cause to indict for criminal homicide?

Yes.
First, the Medical Examiner
for the City of New York
conducted an autopsy and
concluded cause of death was
homicide — in other words, that
the death was caused by the
acts of one or more other
human beings.
       Second, the ME ruled Mr. Garner's
       death was caused by "compression of neck

         (choke hold)

       compression of chest and prone positioning
       during physical restraint by police."

The ME report, which we have
physically seen, specifically
states "compression of the neck

       (chokehold)."

The compression of Garner's neck was around his windpipe,
        causing the asphyxiation, a result of
Pantaleo's
arm around his neck. (Whether it was technically
        a 'chokehold' is in dispute,
with Officer Pantaleo claiming it was a "take down
maneuver."

What is clear from the video is that
Officer Pantaleo put his arm
around Mr. Garner's neck and that
Mr. Garner stated that he could not
breathe while Officer Pantaleo applied
neck and chest compression.

Third, video evidence suggests, and the ME
report confirms, that there
was strong pressure applied to Garner's
neck, characteristic of a

        "chokehold."

Pressure was applied around the neck
of Mr. Garner by Officer Pantaleo.

The video evidence shows that at
the outset of the encounter between
Mr. Garner and the five officers,
Officer Pantaleo used force applied

to his neck area to subdue
Mr. Garner while placing him on
the ground. Once subdued, the video

shows Officer Pantaleo continued to apply
force using a chokehold to Mr. Garner while
he was on the ground. Throughout this time,
both before and after
Mr. Garner was on the ground,

he repeatedly said

"I can't breathe."

He said this audibly 11 times
during the encounter before
Mr. Garner lost consciousness.

Although Officer Pantaleo was permitted
by law to "reasonably" use "necessary force"
to effectuate the arrest of Mr. Garner, once
Mr. Garner was on the ground and subdued,
and while he repeatedly stated that he could
not breathe, the continued use of force was
objectively unreasonable.

In this case, once the suspect was
subdued and no longer resisting,
the continued application of force
may have become unreasonable.

2. The Verdict

I first want to express my
condolences to Eric Garner's
family for their loss, and to
acknowledge the heartache
of his mother, his wife, his children,
as well as his other family members,
loved ones, and friends, who have
consistently carried themselves with grace.

A Richmond County grand jury
has completed its investigation
into the tragic death of Eric Garner
July 17, 2014, after being taken
into police custody for an alleged
sale of untaxed cigarettes.

After deliberation on the evidence
presented in this matter, the grand
jury found that there was no
reasonable cause to vote an indictment.

— Part 1 found from "Questions and Answers for Columbia Law School
Students about the Richmond County (Staten Island) Grand Jury in the Eric
Garner Homicide" By Professors Jeffrey Fagan and Bernard E. Harcourt
Columbia Law School (This Fact Sheet supplements the December 1, 2014,
Fact Sheet on Grand Juries and addresses the decision of the Staten Island

Grand Jury to no-bill the indictment of NYPD Officer Daniel Pantaleo in the homicide of Eric Garner on July 17, 2014.)

– Part 2 found poem from "Statement by Richmond County District Attorney Daniel M. Donovan, Jr., Regarding the No True Bill in The Matter of the Investigation into the Death of Eric Garner".

No Violation – a found poem

– for Victor Steen

given the speed – and
distance   involved in the
crash, it was

        physically

          impossible

for Pensacola
        police officer   Jerald
Ard   to
stop   his patrol car   and avoid
          hitting
          Steen

who was on a bicycle

– found from "Florida Cop Kills 17-year-old Kid" by Ademo Freeman

No Charges to Be Filed in Shooting Near U.S. Capitol – a found poem

– for Miriam Carey

After the shooting and after Ms. Carey's vehicle
crashed into the kiosk and came to rest, the
officers on the scene discovered that there was
a young child in the vehicle. They carried the

child from the car. The child, who was not seriously
injured, was taken to a hospital. Medical personnel
arrived on the scene attempted to revive Ms. Carey.
She was transported to a hospital,

where she was pronounced dead. Ms. Carey
sustained five gunshot wounds to her neck
and torso area, one of which was fatal. She was not
under the influence of illegal drugs or alcohol, and no

weapon was recovered from inside her vehicle.
Under the applicable federal criminal civil rights
laws, prosecutors must establish beyond a reasonable
doubt not only that an officer's use of force was

excessive, but also that the officer willfully deprived
an individual of a constitutional right. Proving
"willfulness" is a heavy burden, and means that it
must be proven that the officer acted with the

deliberate and specific intent to do something the
law forbids. Accident, mistake, fear, negligence
and bad judgment do not establish such a criminal
violation. After a careful, thorough and independent

review of the evidence, federal prosecutors have
found insufficient evidence to prove beyond a
reasonable doubt that these officers used excessive
force under the circumstances known to them at the

time or that they acted with the requisite criminal intent.

Accordingly, the investigation into this incident has been
closed without prosecution.

– found from "FOR IMMEDIATE RELEASE Thursday, July 10, 2014
U.S. Attorney's Office Concludes Investigation Into The Death Of Miriam
Carey No Charges To Be Filed In Shooting Near U.S. Capitol" by the
Department of Justice U.S. Attorney's Office District of Columbia

The Bodies Speak

Here I include excerpts of the autopsies I could collect in order to find some way that those murdered by police could speak since their lives were taken unexpectedly. The only poem in this section then, is a poem titled "Imagine: a love song" in the voice of Sandra Bland whose videos about police brutality and race well before her death gave me a sense of her voice.

Laquan McDonald
REPORT OF POSTMORTEM EXAMINATION

The body is identified by toe tag. Photographs and radiographs are taken. When first viewed, the body is clad in a green hospital gown. A tan rubber band encircles the right wrist. Accompanying the body is a black, hooded, zip-up sweatshirt (cut), a black with white lettering sweatshirt, blue jeans, black boxers (cut), two black shoes and two black socks. No jewelry is present. All of the clothing is relinquished to a representative of the Chicago Police Department.

The body is that of a well-developed, well-nourished, black male whose appearance is compatible with the stated age of 17 years.

The black scalp hair is in dreadlocks up to 5 inches long. An average amount of body hair is in a normal male distribution. The irides are brown, the corneae are clear, and there are no petechiae of the bulbar or palpebral surfaces of the conjunctivae. The ears, nose and lips are unremarkable. The teeth are natural and in good condition with absence of the upper left central incisor. The neck and chest are symmetrical, and the abdomen is flat. The external genitalia, anus and perineum are unremarkable. The extremities are well developed and symmetrical. The back is straight.

Tamir Rice
AUTOPSY REPORT

The body is identified by Medical Examiners tags attached to both great toes. The body is received in a secured fashion from the hospital.

EXTERNAL EXAMINATION:

The body is of a well developed, well nourished, edematous, 67 inch, 195 pound, black adolescent male...

<u>Injuries, Internal and External:</u> There is a penetrating gunshot wound of the torso. Directions are given on standard anatomical planes.

The recovered bullet is metal jacketed and moderately deformed with mushrooming at the nose. It appears to be of medium caliber and is now inscribed "TR" on the base and submitted to evidence after being photographed.

George Floyd
AUTOPSY REPORT

FINAL DIAGNOSES: 46-year-old man who became unresponsive while being restrained by law enforcement officers; he received emergency medical care in the field and subsequently in the Hennepin HealthCare (HHC) Emergency Department, but could not be resuscitated.

I. Blunt force injuries

    A. Cutaneous blunt force injuries of the forehead, face, and upper lip

    B. Mucosal injuries of the lips

    C. Cutaneous blunt force injuries of the shoulders, hands, elbows, and legs

    D. Patterned contusions (in some areas abraded) of the wrists, consistent with restraints (handcuffs)

Sandra Bland
AUTOPSY REPORT

Received in the body bag with the decedent Is a paper bag
labeled "Trash Bag Used as Ligature:

PATHOLOGICAL FINDINGS

I. Hanging

    A. Ligature furrow around neck

    B. Internal examination negative for neck
musculature hemorrhages

    C. Internal examination negative for fractures of
hyoid bone, thyroid cartilage, cricoid cartilage and
cervical vertebrae

    D. Investigative information indicates the decedent
was found hanging from a beam in her solitary jail
cell by a ligature made of a transparent white plastic
trash bag

    E. Ligature (plastic trash bag) recovered and
submitted as evidence

II. Healing superficial parallel horizontal incised wounds
numbering approximately 25-30 of volar left forearm

III. Healing superficial blunt injuries
    A. Healing abrasions and contusions, right upper back and shoulder
    B. Healing abrasions and contusions, right elbow region
    C. Healing contusion, left forearm
    Healing abrasions and contusions, bilateral wrists

Imagine: A Love Song

– for and "from" Sandra Bland

Imagine I am not fingernail scrapings – imagine

I
am not neck, or vagina or legs – Imagine I,
am not a knot.
Imagine you are not a toe tag. Not rubber band that
encircles the right wrist. Not a black hooded,
zip-up sweatshirt (cut) black – Not black
with white lettering, blue jeans, black – boxers
(cut), two black –   shoes   and two black –
socks.

Imagine you   are
not tags
attached to both great toes – ankles tied
together – a boy altered by surgical
intervention – Imagine you are not
a recovered bullet, metal jacketed moderately deformed,
          mushrooming
at the nose – Now "TR"
          inscribed on its base

Imagine you are not a no-knock warrant –
not   a   headline.
Not a 26-year-old first-responder   not bullet
battered in the hallway of your home.

Imagine you are not a case title:
cardiopulmonary arrest complicating law enforcement
subdual, restraint,   neck compression.
            Imagine you are not evidence, labeled in a
locked body bag —

Imagine? Instead? —
We —
 are not

kidney, or head, or hands. Imagine we — are not
unremarkable, not — skin as thin or disposable
or ordinary as a plastic garbage bag.

Imagine us
not on display
not   pathology
                        or pathologized

Imagine We —
backs, still vertical — still alive. Not

            twisted until   made lethal.

Afterward

Dear Spectators 2, A Bed Time Story

He is menacing she is angry he is big she is
screaming he is raping she is running he is
she is he is she is he is she is he is

they are —

black trees falling in a black forest — cut down
by the axed tongue of a nation's origin that's more
myth than story. If you want me to tuck you
in at bed time, I will tell you about Old Glory.

She was conceived by conjurers egged and spermed
by white whaled wanderers who wandered wayless
on seas so high they lost their way and called it
discovering. Then she was birthed fiber twisted

and fixed by hands so quick to thimble her, they left
her red and white and hovering — afterbirth fluttering
in wind so thin she was left mothering the blue-bruised
female, brown, and black bodies they'd begun fucking

since well before they got here. Well, before they got
here they'd already cracked open whole countries and
continents sharpened humans into soldiers sharpened
soldiers into armies sharpened armies into the teeth

of a mouth that gorged on their contents and still they
were not content, not full, not satiated. Fast forward
almost twelve score and more years to: *He is raping she
is angry he is big she is screaming he is running she is he is*

she is he they all become headlines. From a Virginia
runaway advertisement to a current news story about
the background of another dead black body even before
their blood stops stippling pavement, black and brown

people's stories have been spun so quickly and so thoroughly so
that suddenly our lives seem to justify the ending of them. Black
and brown bodies have been named from auctions blocks to
blogs and back again as   *those people* for centuries; and that

identity created and written by people who would lynch, police
officers who would shoot to kill and judges and juries who would
acquit, has been fatal. This is not new. But some of you want
a child friendly bed time story, get comfortable, tuck in

and let them wrap up in Old Glory — then scroll down.
See a picture of a black boy or black girl, a black man or
a black woman, a black person or a black person and you
wonder is she or isn't she, is he or isn't he, are they

or aren't they and each isn't but each is, you wonder is it another
story of or isn't it? You wonder is it a graduation or is it the grave?
Are they another hashtag or are they the college graduate whose
college acceptance is like the exhale of a pitcher's save

at the bottom of the 9th See you want to exhale, you'd rather
exhale because digging deep is not what you want to do right now.
You'd rather slide finger up screen like eraser across slate, scroll
the past the hate as if it's not been sown into the fabric of your

pillow, scroll past as if the weeping willow wrapped around a
brown neck isn't the dream catcher we always wake to, scroll past
the white police officer whose dream it is to catch and rape her
scroll past as if this story isn't ours but it is – see we have

moved way beyond old glory to
he is raping she is angry he is big she is
screaming he is running she is
He is she is he is she is he is she is

He was 12
She was 37
He was 19
She was 34
He was 18
She was 47
He was 26
She was 16
He was 6
She was 22
He was 22
She was 26
He was 19
She was 55

He was 46

She was 7

He was 23

She was 3

He was 17

She was 15

He was 13

She was human

He was human

She was breathing

He was breathing

She was

He was

She was

He was

She was

He was

She was

He was

They were.